And It Was Good

And It Was Good

Illustrated by

HAROLD HORST NOFZIGER

Text based on the NRSV Bible

HERALD PRESS
Scottdale, Pennsylvania
Waterloo, Ontario

In the beginning
  when God created
  the heavens and the earth,
darkness covered
  the face of the deep.

Then God said,
  "Let there be light";
and there was light.

And God saw
  that the light was good.

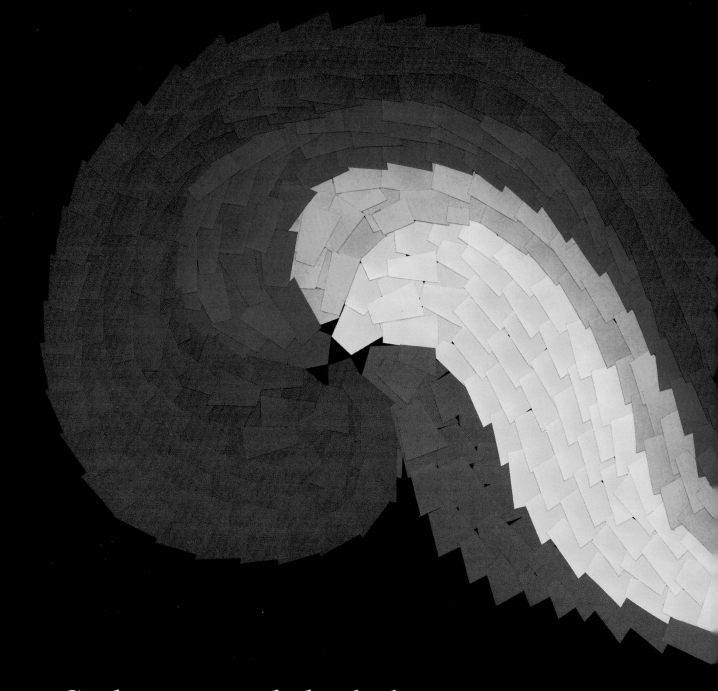

God separated the light
  from the darkness.
God called the light Day,
  and the darkness he called Night.

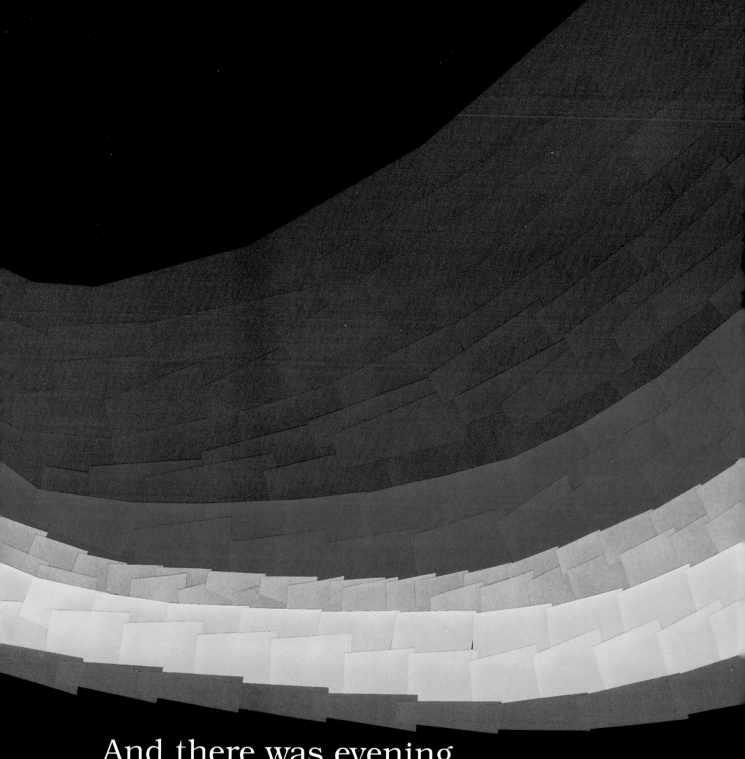

And there was evening
and there was morning,
the first day.

God separated the waters
that were under the dome
from the waters above the dome.
God called the dome Sky.

And there was evening
and there was morning,
the second day.

And God said,
  "Let the waters under the sky
  be gathered together in one place,
  and let the dry land appear."

God called
  the dry land Earth.

And the waters
   that were gathered together
   he called Seas.

And God saw
   that it was good.

The earth brought forth vegetation:
  plants of every kind
  and trees of every kind.

And God saw
  that it was good.

And there was evening
and there was morning,
  the third day.

And God said,
   "Let there be lights in the sky
   to separate the day from the night."

God made two lights—
   the greater light
   to rule the day

And the lesser light
   to rule the night—
   and the stars.

And God saw
   that it was good.

And there was evening
and there was morning,
   the fourth day.

And God said,
  "Let the waters bring forth
  swarms of living creatures."

So God created
  the great sea monsters
  and every living creature
  with which the waters swarm.

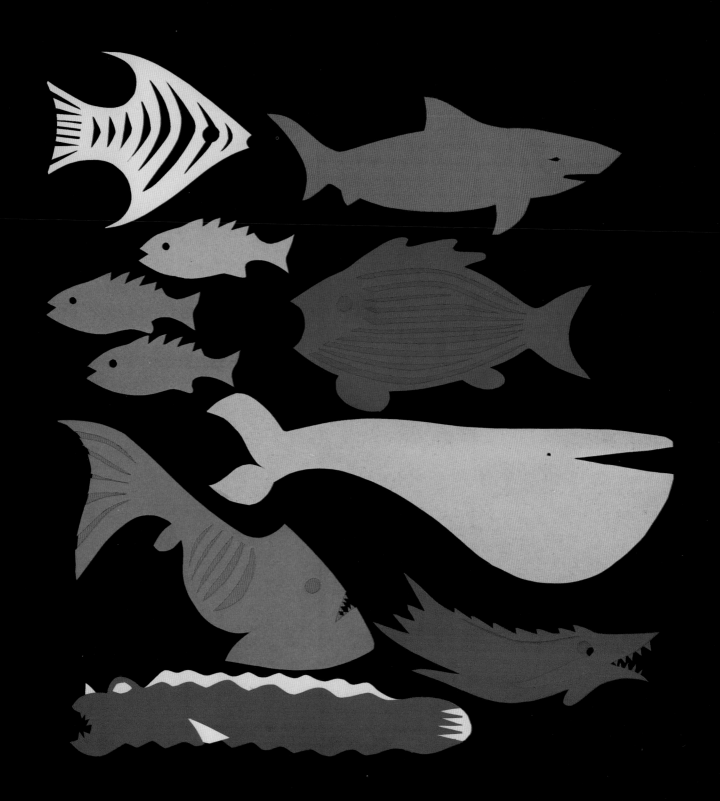

And God said,
  "Let birds fly above the earth."
So God created
  every winged bird of every kind.

And God saw
  that it was good.

And there was evening
and there was morning,
  the fifth day.

And God said,
   "Let the earth bring forth
   living creatures of every kind."

God made
   the wild animals of the earth
   of every kind,

And the cattle of every kind,

And everything that creeps
    upon the ground.

And God saw
    that it was good.

Then God said,
   "Let us make humankind
   in our image."

Male and female
   he created them.

God blessed them,
and God said,
  "Fill the earth
  and subdue it;
  and have dominion
  over every living thing."

God saw everything
  that he had made,
and indeed, it was very good.

And on the seventh day
   God finished the work
   that he had done,
and he rested
   on the seventh day.

Library of Congress Cataloging-in-Publication Data
Bible. O.T. Genesis I-II, 4. English. New Revised Standard. 1993.
  And it was good : text based on the NRSV Bible / illustrated by
Harold Horst Nofziger.
    p.   cm.
  Summary: Tells the Old Testament story of God's creation of the
world.
  ISBN 0-8361-3634-9 (hardcover : alk. paper)
  [1. Creation.] I. Nofziger, Harold Horst, 1951-   ill.
II. Title
BS1233.N648 1993
222'.110520434—dc20   93-19336
                                                             CIP
                                                              AC

The paper used in this publication is recycled and meets the
minimum requirements of American National Standard for
Information Sciences—Permanence of Paper for Printed Library
Materials, ANSI Z39.48-1984.

02 01 00 99 98 97 96 95 94 93 10 9 8 7 6 5 4 3 2 1

The Illustrator

Harold Horst Nofziger was born in Hannibal, Missouri, and grew up in Kansas, Georgia, and the Sudan. After graduating from Hesston (Kan.) College in 1972, he worked as a studio potter for Koinonia Partners, taught skills for job training to mentally handicapped children and for independent living to handicapped adults, and completed college with honors in computer science.

Nofziger is employed as a senior programmer analyst. He also enjoys working in various art media: painting, freehand sketching, printmaking, and cut paper—as in the original art for this book. Harold is a member of Pilgrim Mennonite Church of Akron, Pennsylvania, and lives in Lancaster (Pa.) with his wife, Phyllis, and two sons.